OKLAHOMA GUN LAWS

Don't panic!
Call Urbanic.®

Frank A. Urbanic, Esq.

ISBN: 978-1-946481-42-9

Designed and Published by:

Speakeasy Publications
73-03 Bell Blvd, #10
Oakland Gardens, NY 11364
www.SpeakeasyMarketingInc.com
888-225-8594

DISCLAIMER

This publication is intended to be informational only. No legal advice is being given, and no attorney-client relationship is intended to be created by reading this material. If you are facing legal issues, whether criminal or civil, seek professional legal counsel to get your questions answered. The law cited is current as of September 1, 2018. Laws are subject to change at any time.

THE URBANIC LAW FIRM, PLLC
1141 N Robinson Avenue
Suite 101
Oklahoma City, OK 73103
(405) 633-3420

Frank@Urbanic.Law

www.Urbanic.Law

TABLE OF CONTENTS

About Frank Urbanic

I became a criminal defense attorney because I'm intimately familiar with how precious our constitutional rights are. After my arrest years ago, I realized how close I was to being in a situation that could have negatively impacted my life forever. That experience made me realize how important it is to have someone on your side who feels strongly about protecting your rights.

In the Air Force, I put my life on the line to support and defend the Constitution during combat. Today, I support and defend the Constitution in the courtroom. My legal career began by representing indigent clients. I saw first-hand how important it is for everyone to have legal representation.

Through my extensive business training at The University of Oklahoma and Texas A&M University, I've learned proven business techniques that allow me to operate a lean and efficient law firm. These techniques include document automation, checklists, templates, the use of cutting-edge technology, and continuous process improvement practices. My firm uses these business techniques to produce high-quality legal representation in a fraction of the time. Less waste means more value to my clients.

While many offices are still dealing with paper folders, we are digital. No missing documents. No messy folders. Using cloud-based technology, I can work on your case from anywhere on the planet. Whether I'm in a Starbucks or in an airplane at 30,000 ft, I'm still able to work on cases.

What Makes The Urbanic Law Firm Suited To Defend Your Rights

- Extensive Experience In Handling Criminal Defense Cases
- Rated Superb On AVVO.com
- Employing Cutting-Edge Technology To The Benefit Of Our Clients
- Providing High-Quality Criminal Defense At A Reasonable Price
- Intensive Criminal Defense Training In The Caprock Regional Public Defender Office

My Firm Has Handled Cases In The Following Areas

- Criminal Defense
- DUI, DWI, & APC
- Domestic Assault & Battery
- Theft Crimes
- Drug Possession, Distribution, and Trafficking
- Firearms offenses

Additional Training

- Standardized Field Sobriety Test (SFST) Instructor
- Standardized Field Sobriety Test (SFST) Practitioner
- Advanced Roadside Impaired Driving Enforcement (ARIDE) Practitioner
- Drug Recognition Expert (DRE) Overview Course graduate
- Oklahoma State Bureau of Investigation Forensics Academy graduate

Professional Associations And Memberships

- National Association of Criminal Defense Lawyers
- National College for DUI Defense
- Oklahoma Criminal Defense Lawyers Association
- Oklahoma Bar Association
- Oklahoma County Bar Association
- Canadian County Bar Association
- Oklahoma County Criminal Defense Lawyers Association
- Order of the Coif

- Phi Kappa Phi
- Lead Counsel Rated

Books

- DUI In Oklahoma
- Oklahoma Drug Laws
- Domestic Violence & Victim Protective Orders In Oklahoma
- Theft, Burglary, & Robbery In Oklahoma

Bar Admissions

- Oklahoma

Can I Possess A Gun In Oklahoma?

It's illegal for felons, delinquents, youthful offenders, and intoxicated people to possess a firearm in Oklahoma. It's illegal for minors to possess firearms in certain circumstances.

Felons & Delinquents In Possession Of A Firearm

The statute that covers convicted felons and delinquents is 21 O.S. § 1283. It's illegal for:

- A felon to have any pistol, imitation or homemade pistol, altered air or toy pistol, machine gun, sawed-off shotgun or rifle, or any other dangerous or deadly firearm in his or her possession, under his or her immediate control, in any vehicle that he or she is operating or riding in as a passenger, or at the residence where the felon resides. This is commonly referred to as "Felon in Possession of a Firearm" or "Possession of a Firearm AFCF (After Former Conviction of a Felony)";
- Anyone on felony probation or under the jurisdiction of any alternative court program to possess; have under his or her immediate control; or have at his or her residence or in any passenger vehicle that the

person is operating or is riding as a passenger any pistol, shotgun, or rifle. This includes any imitation or homemade pistol, altered air or toy pistol, shotgun, or rifle. This applies while the person is subject to supervision, probation, parole, or inmate status; and

- Someone to possess a firearm if he or she has been adjudicated as a delinquent child or as a youthful offender for committing an offense that would have constituted a felony offense if committed by an adult.

It's a felony to commit any of the above violations. The range of punishment in the Department of Corrections is one–ten years.

"Sawed-off shotgun or rifle" means any shotgun or rifle that has been shortened to any length. "Altered toy pistol" means any toy weapon that has been altered from its original manufactured state to resemble a real weapon. "Altered air pistol" means any air pistol manufactured to propel projectiles by air pressure that's been altered from its original manufactured state. "Alternative court program" means any drug court, Anna McBride or mental health court, DUI court, or veterans court.

SOURCES: 21 O.S. § 1283 & 21 O.S. § 1284

Can A Minor Possess A Firearm In Oklahoma?

It's a violation of 21 O.S. § 1273 for any child to possess any pistol, revolver, shotgun or rifle (whether loaded or unloaded), blackjack, loaded cane, billy, hand chain, metal knuckles, or any other offensive weapon. However, a minor can legally possess firearms used for participation in hunting animals or fowl, hunter safety classes, education and training in the safe use and handling of firearms, target shooting, skeet, trap, or other sporting events or competitions. The exceptions don't authorize the possession of a firearm by someone otherwise prohibited from possessing it.

This crime is a misdemeanor. The maximum punishment for the first violation is 30 days in the county jail, and the range of fine is $100–$250. On the second and subsequent violations, the range of fine is $250–$500, and the range of punishment in the county jail is 30 days–3 months.

Any child who violates this law is subject to adjudication as a delinquent. A "child" is a person under 18 years old.

SOURCES: 21 O.S. § 1273, 21 O.S. § 1272, 21 O.S. § 1276, & 23 O.S. § 10

Carrying Weapon Under The Influence Of Alcohol

It's a violation of 21 O.S. § 1289.9 to carry or use shotguns, rifles, or pistols in any circumstances while under the influence of beer, intoxicating liquors, any hallucinogenic, or any unlawful or un-prescribed drug. It's also illegal to carry or use shotguns, rifles, or pistols when under the influence of any drug prescribed by a licensed physician if the aftereffects of such consumption affect mental, emotional, or physical processes to a degree that would result in abnormal behavior.

This crime is a misdemeanor. The range of punishment in the county jail is ten days–six months. The range of fine is $50–$500.

Anyone convicted of violating this law after having been issued a handgun license pursuant to the Oklahoma Self-Defense Act will have his or her license suspended for six months and will be subject to an administrative fine of $50. Prior to the suspension and fine, there must be a hearing and determination by the OSBI that the person violated this law.

SOURCES: 21 O.S. § 1289.9 & 21 O.S. § 1289.15

Restoration Of Gun Rights

Anyone who has previously been convicted of a nonviolent felony, received a full and complete pardon from the proper authority, and has not been convicted of any other felony offense that has not been pardoned will have restored their right to:

1. Possess any lawful firearm or other weapon;
2. Apply for and carry a handgun, concealed or unconcealed, pursuant to the Oklahoma Self-Defense Act; and
3. Perform the duties of a peace officer, gunsmith, or for firearms repair.

SOURCE: 21 O.S. § 1283

WHO CAN I GIVE A GUN TO IN OKLAHOMA?

It's illegal to give firearms to felons, delinquents, youthful offenders, incompetent people, and intoxicated people. It's illegal to give firearms to minors in certain circumstances.

Giving Firearms To Convicted Persons, Delinquents, & People Under The Influence

It's a violation of 21 O.S. § 1289.12 to knowingly sell, trade, give, transmit, or otherwise cause the transfer of rifles, shotguns, or pistols to any convicted felon or an adjudicated delinquent. It's also illegal to knowingly sell, trade, give, transmit, or otherwise cause the transfer of any shotgun, rifle, or pistol to any individual who is under the influence of alcohol or drugs or is mentally or emotionally unbalanced or disturbed. Anyone who engages in selling, trading, or otherwise transferring firearms must display this law prominently in full view at or near the point of normal firearms sale, trade, or transfer.

This crime is a misdemeanor. The range of punishment in

the county jail is ten days–six months. The range of fine is $50–$500.

Anyone convicted of violating this law after having been issued a handgun license pursuant to the Oklahoma Self-Defense Act will have his or her license suspended for six months and will be subject to an administrative fine of $50. Prior to the suspension and fine, there must be a hearing and determination by the OSBI that the person violated this law.

SOURCES: 21 O.S. § 1289.12 & 21 O.S. § 1289.15

Concealed Handgun License Holders Giving Pistol To Felons, Delinquents, Or Youthful Offenders

It's a violation of 21 O.S. § 1283 for someone who was issued a handgun license pursuant to the Oklahoma Self-Defense Act to knowingly or intentionally allow a convicted felon, adjudicated delinquent, or youthful offender to possess or have control of any pistol authorized by the Oklahoma Self-Defense Act.

This crime is a felony. The range of punishment in the Department of Corrections is one–ten years. The maximum fine is $5,000. Additionally, the person's handgun license will be revoked by the OSBI after a hearing and determination that the person has violated this law.

SOURCES: 21 O.S. § 1283 & 21 O.S. § 1284

Giving Firearms To Incompetent Persons

It's a violation of 21 O.S. § 1289.10 to knowingly transmit, transfer, sell, lend, or furnish any shotgun, rifle, or pistol to any person who is under an adjudication of mental incompetency, mentally deficient, or of unsound mind.

This crime is a misdemeanor. The range of punishment in the county jail is ten days–six months. The range of fine is $50–$500.

Anyone convicted of violating this law after having been issued a handgun license pursuant to the Oklahoma Self-Defense Act will have his or her license suspended for a term of six months and will be subject to an administrative fine of $50. Prior to the suspension and fine, there must be a hearing and determination by the OSBI that the person is in violation of this law.

SOURCES: 21 O.S. § 1289.10 & 21 O.S. § 1289.15

Giving A Firearm To A Minor

It's a violation of 21 O.S. § 1273 to sell or give to any child any pistol, revolver, shotgun or rifle (whether loaded or unloaded), blackjack, loaded cane, billy, hand chain, metal knuckles, or any other offensive weapon. However, there is no prohibition on a parent of a child, legal guardian of a child, or a person acting with the permission of the parent or legal guardian of the child from giving the child a firearm for participation in hunting animals or fowl, hunter safety classes, education and training in the safe use and handling of firearms, target shooting, skeet, trap, or other sporting events or competitions. It's illegal for any parent or guardian to intentionally, knowingly, or recklessly permit his or her child to possess any of the arms or weapons previously mentioned if the parent is aware of a substantial risk that the child will use the weapon to commit a criminal offense or if the child has either been adjudicated a delinquent or has been convicted as an adult for any criminal offense that contains the threat or use of physical force against someone as an element.

Any person who sells, gives, or allows their child to possess any pistol, revolver, shotgun or rifle (whether loaded or unloaded), blackjack, loaded cane, billy, hand chain, metal knuckles, or any other offensive weapon will be liable for civil damages for any injury or death to any person and for any damage to property, per 23 O.S. § 10, resulting from any discharge of a firearm by the child or use of any other weapon that the person had given to the child or permitted the child to possess.

This crime is a misdemeanor. The maximum punishment for the first violation is 30 days in the county jail. The range of fine is $100–$250. On the second and subsequent violations, the range of fine is $250–$500, and the range of punishment in the county jail is 30 days–3 months.

Anyone convicted of violating this law after having been issued a handgun license pursuant to the Oklahoma Self-Defense Act will have their license suspended for a period of six months and will be liable for an administrative fine of $50 upon a hearing and determination by the OSBI that the person is in violation of this section.

Any child violating this law is subject to adjudication as a delinquent. A "child" is a person under 18 years old.

SOURCES: 21 O.S. § 1273, 21 O.S. § 1272, 21 O.S. § 1276, & 23 O.S. § 10

DIFFERENCE BETWEEN CONCEALED AND OPEN CARRY IN OKLAHOMA

A concealed handgun is a loaded or unloaded pistol or handgun that's not openly visible to the ordinary observation of a reasonable person.

An unconcealed handgun—or "open carry"—means a loaded or unloaded pistol or handgun carried upon the person in a holster where the firearm is visible or carried upon the person in using a scabbard, sling, or case designed for carrying firearms.

A "pistol" or "handgun" means any derringer, revolver, or semiautomatic firearm that:

- Has an overall barrel or barrels length of less than 16";
- Is capable of discharging single or multiple projectiles from a single round of ammunition composed of any material that may reasonably be expected to be able to cause lethal injury;
- Can be held and fired by the use of one or both hands; and
- Uses a combustible propellant charge to propel the projectile(s).

The definition of pistol or handgun for purposes of the Oklahoma Self-Defense Act doesn't apply to imitation pistols, flare guns, underwater fishing guns, or blank pistols.

SOURCE: 21 O.S. § 1290.2

What Kind Of Firearms Can Be Carried In Oklahoma?

The statute that outlines the conditions under which it is unlawful to carry a firearm is 21 O.S. § 1272. Pistols and handguns are defined in 21 O.S. § 1289.3. Rifles are defined in 21 O.S. § 1289.4. Shotguns are defined in 21 O.S. § 1289.5. The conditions under which a person may legally carry loaded and unloaded shotguns, rifles, and pistols not concealed and without a handgun license are in 21 O.S. § 1289.6.

It's a violation of 21 O.S. § 1272 for someone to carry upon or about his or her person, or in a purse or other container belonging to the person, any pistol, revolver, shotgun or rifle (whether loaded or unloaded), blackjack, loaded cane, billy, hand chain, metal knuckles, or any other offensive weapon, whether such weapon is concealed or unconcealed, except this law doesn't prohibit:

1. The proper use of guns and knives for hunting, fishing, educational, or recreational purposes;
2. The carrying or use of weapons in a manner otherwise permitted by statute or authorized by the Oklahoma Self-Defense Act;
3. The carrying, possession, and use of any weapon by a peace officer or other person authorized by law to carry a weapon in the performance of official duties and in compliance with the rules of the employing agency;
4. The carrying or use of weapons in a courthouse by a district judge, associate district judge, or special district judge within Oklahoma, who is in possession of a valid handgun license issued pursuant to the Oklahoma Self-Defense Act and whose name appears on a list maintained by the Administrative Director of the Courts; or
5. The carrying and use of firearms and other weapons provided in this statute when used for living history reenactment. "Living history reenactment" means the depiction of historical characters, scenes, historical life, or events for entertainment, education, or historical documentation through the wearing or use of period, historical, antique or vintage clothing, accessories, firearms, weapons, and other implements

of the historical period.

Succinctly, carrying a gun without a permit and not otherwise authorized in this law is illegal.

This crime is a misdemeanor. The maximum punishment for the first violation is in 30 days in the county jail, and the range of fine is $100–$250. On the second and subsequent violations, the range of punishment in the county jail is 30 days–3 months, and the range of fine is $250–$500.

Any person convicted of violating this law after having been issued a handgun license pursuant to the Oklahoma Self-Defense Act will have their license suspended for a period of six months and will be liable for an administrative fine of $50. There must first be a hearing and determination by the OSBI that the person violated this law.

"Pistols" or "handguns" mean any firearm capable of discharging single or multiple projectiles from a single round of ammunition composed of any material that may reasonably be expected to be able to cause lethal injury. The barrel or barrels must be less than 16" long. There must be a combustible propellant charge. This doesn't include flare guns, underwater fishing guns, or blank pistols.

"Rifles" means any firearm capable of discharging a projectile composed of any material that may reasonably be expected to be able to cause lethal injury. The barrel or barrels must be more than 16" inches long. It must use either gunpowder, gas, or any means of rocket propulsion. This does not include archery equipment, flare guns, or underwater fishing guns. Any rifle capable of firing "shot" but primarily designed to fire single projectiles is regarded as a "rifle."

"Shotguns" means any firearm capable of discharging a series of projectiles of any material that may reasonably be expected to be able to cause lethal injury. The barrel or barrels must be more than 18" long. It must use either gunpowder, gas, or any means of rocket propulsion. This does not include any weapon so designed with a barrel less than 18" long. Any "shotgun" capable of firing single projectiles but primarily designed to fire multiple projectiles such as "shot" is regarded as a "shotgun."

SOURCES: 21 O.S. § 1272, 21 O.S. § 1276, 21 O.S. § 1289.3, 21 O.S. § 1289.4, & 21 O.S. § 1289.5

Requirements To Legally Carry A Handgun In Oklahoma

The statute that outlines the eligibility for legally carrying a handgun in Oklahoma is 21 O.S. § 1290.8. It states that you have the authority to carry a concealed or unconcealed handgun in Oklahoma when you are not otherwise prohibited by law and:

1. You have been issued a handgun license from the OSBI pursuant to the Oklahoma Self-Defense Act, provided that you are in compliance with the Oklahoma Self-Defense Act, and the license has not expired or been subsequently suspended or revoked; or
2. You are 21 years old or older, and are either
   a. active military; or
   b. a member of the Reserve or National Guard (to include Drill Status Guard and Reserve), Active Guard Reserves, or a Military Technician and present a valid military identification card, which will be considered a valid handgun license issued pursuant to the Oklahoma Self-Defense Act.

A person in possession of a valid handgun license or who

meets the criteria and presents a valid military identification card as provided for in this law and in compliance with the Oklahoma Self-Defense Act is authorized to carry a concealed or unconcealed handgun while bow hunting or fishing.

You must have possession of your valid handgun license or valid military identification card and a valid Oklahoma driver license or an Oklahoma State photo identification at all times when in possession of an authorized pistol. You must display the handgun license, or a valid military identification card, upon the demand of a law enforcement officer; provided, however, that in the absence of reasonable and articulable suspicion of other criminal activity, you can't be disarmed or physically restrained unless the you fail to display a valid handgun license or a valid military identification card in response to that demand.

A violation of this law is a misdemeanor. The maximum punishment for the first violation is 30 days in the county jail. The range of fine is \$100–\$250. On the second and subsequent violations, the range of punishment in the county jail is 30 days–3 months, and the range of fine is \$250–\$500.

Any second or subsequent violation of 21 O.S. § 1290.8 is grounds for the OSBI to suspend the handgun license for a period of six months, in addition to any other penalty imposed.

SOURCES: 21 OS § 1290.8, 21 O.S. § 1272, & 21 O.S. § 1276

REQUIREMENTS TO APPLY FOR A HANDGUN LICENSE IN OKLAHOMA

The eligibility requirements for someone to get a handgun license are in 21 O.S. § 1290.9. You must:

1. Be a citizen of the United States;
2. Establish a residency in the State of Oklahoma. For purposes of the Oklahoma Self-Defense Act, the term "residency" applies to any person who either possesses a valid Oklahoma driver license, or state photo identification card, and physically maintains a residence in Oklahoma. It also applies to any person, including the spouse of such person, who has permanent military orders within Oklahoma and possesses a valid drivers license from another state where the person and spouse of that person claim residency;

3. Be at least:
   a. 21 years old or
   b. 18 years old but not yet 21 years old and be a member or veteran of the United States Armed Forces, the Reserves, or National Guard, or have been discharged under honorable conditions from the United States Armed Forces, Reserves, or

National Guard;

4. Complete a firearms safety and training course, demonstrate competence and qualifications with the type of pistol to be carried, and submit proof of training and qualification or an exemption for training and qualification;
5. Submit the required fee and complete the application process; and
6. Comply in good faith with the Oklahoma Self-Defense Act.

SOURCES: 21 O.S. § 1290.9, 21 O.S. § 1290.12, & 21 O.S. § 1290.14

WHAT MAKES SOMEONE INELIGIBLE FOR A GUN LICENSE IN OKLAHOMA?

The occurrence of any one of the following prohibited conditions, listed in 21 O.S. § 1290.10, will deny someone the right to have an Oklahoma gun license:

1. Ineligible to possess a pistol due to any felony conviction or adjudication as a delinquent, except for someone who has received a full and complete pardon from the proper authority and has not been convicted of any other felony offense that has not been pardoned;
2. Any felony conviction pursuant to any law of another state, a felony conviction pursuant to any provision of the United States Code, or any conviction pursuant to the laws of any foreign country. If it's a foreign conviction, then the crime must constitute a felony offense in Oklahoma if it had been committed in Oklahoma. Someone who has received a full and complete pardon from the proper authority and has not been convicted of any other felony offense that has not been pardoned is excepted from this section;
3. Adjudication as a mentally incompetent person

pursuant to the Oklahoma Mental Health Law, or an adjudication of incompetency entered in another state pursuant to any law of that state, unless the person has been granted relief from the disqualifying disability;

4. Any false or misleading statement on the application for a handgun license;
5. Conviction of any one of the following misdemeanor offenses in Oklahoma or any other state:
   a. Any assault and battery that caused serious physical injury to the victim or any second or subsequent assault and battery conviction;
   b. Any aggravated assault and battery;
   c. Any stalking pursuant to Oklahoma law or a similar law of another state;
   d. A violation relating to the Protection from Domestic Abuse Act;
   e. Any violation of a victim protection order of another state;
   f. Any conviction relating to illegal drug use or possession. The preclusive period for a misdemeanor conviction related to illegal drug use or possession is ten years from the date of completion of a sentence—the day an offender completes all incarceration, probation, and parole pertaining to that sentence; or

g. An act of domestic abuse or an act of domestic assault and battery or any comparable acts under the laws of another state.

6. An attempted suicide or other condition relating to or indicating mental instability or an unsound mind that occurred within the preceding ten–year period from the date of the application for a license to carry a concealed firearm or that occurs during the period of licensure;
7. Currently undergoing treatment for a mental illness, condition, or disorder. This means that the person has been diagnosed by a licensed physician as being afflicted with a substantial disorder of thought, mood, perception, psychological orientation, or memory that significantly impairs judgment, behavior, capacity to recognize reality, or ability to meet the ordinary demands of life;
8. Significant character defects of the applicant as evidenced by a misdemeanor criminal record indicating habitual criminal activity;
9. Ineligible to possess a pistol due to any Oklahoma law or the United States Code;
10. Failure to pay an assessed fine or surrender the handgun license as required by a decision by the administrative hearing examiner pursuant to authority

of the Oklahoma Self-Defense Act;

11. Being subject to an outstanding felony warrant issued in Oklahoma, in another state, or by the United States; or
12. Adjudication as a delinquent.

The following conditions will preclude a person from being eligible for a handgun license pursuant to the Oklahoma Self-Defense Act for the respective period of time:

1. An arrest for an alleged commission of a felony offense or a felony charge pending in Oklahoma, pending another state, or pursuant to the United States Code. The preclusive period is until the final determination of the matter;
2. The person is on a felony deferred sentence or prosecution in Oklahoma, in another state, or pursuant to federal authority. The preclusive period is three years and begins upon the final determination of the matter;
3. Any involuntary commitment for a mental illness, condition, or disorder or any involuntary commitment in another state pursuant to any laws of that state. The preclusive period will be permanent as provided by 18 United States Code § 922(g)(4) unless the person has

been granted relief from the disqualifying disability;

4. The person has previously undergone treatment for a mental illness, condition, or disorder that requires medication or supervision. The preclusive period is three years from the last date of treatment or upon presentation of a certified statement from a licensed physician stating that the person is either no longer disabled by any mental or psychiatric illness, condition, or disorder or that the person has been stabilized on medication for ten years or more;
5. Inpatient treatment for substance abuse. The preclusive period is three years from the last date of treatment or upon presentation of a certified statement from a licensed physician stating that the person has been free from substance use for 12 months or more preceding the filing of an application for a handgun license;
6. Two or more public intoxication convictions pursuant to Oklahoma law or a similar law of another state. The preclusive period is three years from the date of the completion of the last sentence;
7. Two or more misdemeanor convictions relating to intoxication or driving under the influence of an intoxicating substance or alcohol. The preclusive period is three years from the date of the completion of

the last sentence, or there must be a certified statement from a licensed physician stating that the person is not in need of substance abuse treatment;

8. A court order for a final Victim Protection Order against the applicant in Oklahoma or another state. The preclusive period is three years from the date of the entry of the final court order or 60 days from the date an order was vacated, canceled, or withdrawn;
9. An adjudicated delinquent or convicted felon residing in the residence of the applicant. The preclusive period is 30 days from the date the person no longer resides in the same residence as the applicant; or
10. An arrest for an alleged commission of, a charge pending for, or the person is subject to the provisions of a deferred prosecution for any one or more of the following misdemeanor offenses in Oklahoma or another state:
    a. Any assault and battery that caused serious physical injury to the victim or any second or subsequent assault and battery;
    b. Any aggravated assault and battery;
    c. Any stalking pursuant to Oklahoma or another state's law;
    d. Any violation of the Protection from Domestic Abuse Act or any violation of a victim protection

order of another state;

e. Any violation relating to illegal drug use or possession; or

f. An act of domestic abuse under Oklahoma law or an act of domestic assault and battery or any comparable acts under the law of another state.

The preclusive period will be until the final determination of the matter. The preclusive period for a person subject to the provisions of a deferred sentence for the six offenses listed above is three years and begins upon the final determination of the matter.

SOURCES: 21 O.S. § 1290.11, 21 O.S. § 1290.27, & 21 O.S. § 1290.10

When Can I Carry A Firearm Without A License In Oklahoma?

Oklahoma's open carry law is 21 O.S. § 1289.6. It states that a person may carry loaded and unloaded shotguns, rifles, and pistols open and not concealed and without a handgun license under to the following conditions:

1. When hunting animals or fowl;
2. During competition in or practicing in a safety or hunter safety class, target shooting, skeet, trap, or other recognized sporting events;
3. During participation in or in preparation for a military function of the state military forces (Oklahoma Army or Air National Guard), Federal Military Reserve, and active military forces. Oklahoma Army or Air National Guard personnel with proper authorization and performing a military function may carry loaded or unloaded and concealed weapons on Oklahoma Military Department facilities in accordance with rules promulgated by the Adjutant General;
4. During participation in or in preparation for a recognized police function of either a municipal, county, or state government as functioning police

officials;

5. During a practice for or a performance for entertainment purposes;
6. For lawful self-defense and self-protection or any other legitimate purpose in or on property that is owned, leased, rented, or otherwise legally controlled by the person; or
7. For any legitimate purpose not in violation of the Oklahoma Firearms Act of 1971 or any legislative enactment regarding the use, ownership, and control of firearms.

A person is allowed to carry unloaded shotguns, rifles, and pistols open and not concealed and without a handgun license under the following conditions:

1. When going to or from the person's private residence or vehicle or a vehicle in which the person is riding as a passenger to a place designated or authorized for: firearms repairs or reconditioning; firearms trade, sale, or barter; gunsmith, hunting animals or fowl; hunter safety course; target shooting; skeet or trap shooting; or any recognized firearms activity or event and while in such places; or
2. For any legitimate purpose not in violation of the Oklahoma Firearms Act of 1971.

This law doesn't prohibit educational or recreational activities, exhibitions, displays, or shows involving the use or display of rifles, shotguns, pistols, or other weapons if the activity is approved by the property owner and sponsor of the activity.

SOURCE: 21 O.S. § 1289.6

WHERE IN OKLAHOMA IS IT ILLEGAL TO CARRY A FIREARM?

The primary statute that controls where people can and can't carry a handgun is 21 O.S. § 1277. The statute that covers carrying a firearm where liquor is consumed is 21 O.S. § 1272.1. The possession of a firearm on school property is covered in 21 O.S. § 1280.1.

Prohibited Places For Carrying A Gun In Oklahoma

According to 21 O.S. § 1277, it's illegal for someone who has a valid handgun license to carry any concealed or unconcealed handgun into any of the following places:

1. Any structure, building, or office space that is owned or leased by a city, town, county, state, or federal governmental authority for the purpose of conducting business with the public;
2. Any courthouse, courtroom, prison, jail, detention facility, or any facility used to process, hold, or house arrested persons, prisoners, or people alleged delinquent or adjudicated delinquent (except as provided in 57 O.S. § 21);
3. Any public or private elementary school or public or

private secondary school, subject to the exceptions below;
4. Any publicly owned or operated sports arena or venue during a professional sporting event, unless allowed by the event holder;
5. Any place where gambling is authorized by law, unless allowed by the property owner; and
6. Any other place specifically prohibited by law.

It's a misdemeanor to violate numbers 2 and 3 from above. The maximum fine is $250.

Someone who violates numbers 1, 4, 5, or 6 from above may be denied entrance onto the property or removed from the property. If the person refuses to leave the property and a peace officer is summoned, the person may be issued a citation for an amount no greater than $250.

Nothing contained in this law authorizes or allows any person in control of any of the six places described above to establish any policy or rule that has the effect of prohibiting any person in lawful possession of a handgun license from possession of a handgun allowable under such license in the five places described below.

The prohibited place does not include—and specifically excludes—the following property:

1. Any property set aside for the use or parking of any vehicle, whether attended or unattended, by a city, town, county, state, or federal governmental authority;
2. Any property set aside for the use or parking of any vehicle, whether attended or unattended, that is open to the public, or by any entity engaged in gambling authorized by law;
3. Any property adjacent to a structure, building, or office space in which concealed or unconcealed weapons are prohibited by this law;
4. Any property designated by a city, town, county, or state governmental authority as a park, recreational area, or fairgrounds; provided, nothing in this paragraph authorizes any entry by a person in possession of a concealed or unconcealed handgun into any structure, building, or office space that is specifically prohibited by any of the six places listed above; and
5. Any property set aside by a public or private elementary or secondary school for the use or parking of any vehicle, whether attended or unattended; provided, however, said handgun must be stored and hidden from view in a locked motor vehicle when the

motor vehicle is left unattended on school property.

SOURCES: 21 O.S. § 1277(A), (B), & (E); & 57 O.S. § 21

Carrying A Weapon Onto Private School Property

A concealed or unconcealed weapon may be carried onto private school property or in any school bus or vehicle used by any private school for transportation of students or teachers by a person who is licensed pursuant to the Oklahoma Self-Defense Act. A policy must have been adopted by the governing entity of the private school that authorizes the carrying and possession of a weapon on private school property or in any school bus or vehicle used by a private school.

A school district's board of education may adopt a policy to authorize the carrying of a handgun onto school property by school personnel specifically designated by the board of education, provided such personnel either: 1) possess a valid armed security guard license as provided for in Oklahoma law; or 2) hold a valid reserve peace officer certification. This will not be construed to restrict authority granted elsewhere in law to carry firearms.

SOURCES: 21 O.S. § 1277(C) & (D), 70 O.S. § 5-149.2, 70 O.S. § 3311, & 59 O.S. § 1750.1

Carrying A Handgun Into A College, University, Or Technology Center School

No person in possession of a valid handgun license issued pursuant to the Oklahoma Self-Defense Act is authorized to carry a handgun into or upon any college, university, or technology center school property. However, the following three areas are not prohibited for people who have a valid handgun license:

1. Any property set aside for the use or parking of any vehicle, whether attended or unattended, provided the handgun is carried or stored as required by law and the handgun is not removed from the vehicle without the prior consent of the college or university president or technology center school administrator while the vehicle is on any college, university, or technology center school property;
2. Any property authorized for possession or use of handguns by college, university, or technology center school policy; and
3. Any property authorized by the written consent of the college or university president or technology center school administrator, provided the written consent is carried with the handgun and the valid handgun license while on college, university, or technology center school property.

The college, university, or technology center school may notify the OSBI within ten days of a violation of this law by a licensee. Upon receipt of a written notification of violation, the OSBI will give a reasonable notice to the licensee and hold a hearing. The licensee may be subject to an administrative fine of $250 and may have the handgun license suspended for three months. This can only happen upon a determination that the licensee has violated this law.

A college, university, or technology center school cannot establish any policy or rule that has the effect of prohibiting any person in lawful possession of a handgun license from possession of a handgun allowable under such license in the three categories of places described above. This law does not limit the authority of any college, university, or technology center school in Oklahoma from taking administrative action against any student for any violation of this law.

SOURCE: 21 O.S. § 1277(F)

Exceptions To Prohibition Against Carrying A Gun Into A Courthouse, Courtroom, Prison, Jail, Detention Facility, Elementary School, Secondary School, College, University, Or Technology Center School

The following are circumstances in which guns may be carried:

1. Any peace officer or any person authorized by law to carry a pistol in the course of employment;
2. District judges, associate district judges, and special district judges, who are in possession of a valid handgun license issued pursuant to the Oklahoma Self-Defense Act and whose names appear on a list maintained by the Administrative Director of the Courts, when acting in the course and scope of employment within the courthouses of Oklahoma;
3. Private investigators with a firearms authorization when acting in the course and scope of employment; and
4. Elected officials of a county, who are in possession of a valid handgun license, may carry a concealed handgun when acting in the performance of their duties within the courthouses of the county in which he or she was elected. These provisions don't allow the elected county official to carry the handgun into a courtroom.

A "motor vehicle" is any automobile, truck, minivan, sports utility vehicle, or motorcycle equipped with a locked accessory container within or affixed to the motorcycle.

SOURCES: 21 O.S. § 1277(G) & (H)

Possession Of Firearm On School Property

It's a violation of 21 O.S. § 1280.1 for any person to have in his or her possession on any public or private school property or while in any school bus or vehicle used by any school for transportation of students or teachers any pistol, revolver, shotgun or rifle (whether loaded or unloaded), blackjack, loaded cane, billy, hand chain, metal knuckles, or any other offensive weapon, except as provided by this or any other law.

This crime is a misdemeanor. The maximum punishment in the county jail is one year. The maximum fine is $250.

Firearms and weapons are allowed on school property and considered lawful in the following circumstances:

1. A gun or knife designed for hunting or fishing purposes kept in a privately-owned vehicle and properly displayed or stored as required by law,

provided such vehicle containing the gun or knife is driven onto school property only to transport a student to and from school and the vehicle doesn't remain unattended on school property;

2. A gun or knife used for the purposes of participating in the Oklahoma Department of Wildlife Conservation certified hunter training education course; any other hunting, fishing, safety, or firearms training courses; a recognized firearms sports event, team shooting program, or competition; or living history reenactment. The course or event must be approved by the principal or chief administrator of the school where the course or event is offered. Any weapon must be properly displayed or stored as required by law pending participation in the course, event, program, or competition;
3. Weapons in the possession of any peace officer or other person authorized by law to possess a weapon in the performance of his or her duties and responsibilities;
4. A concealed or unconcealed weapon carried onto private school property or in any school bus or vehicle used by any private school for transportation of students or teachers by a person with a valid handgun license. The governing entity of the private school

must first adopt a policy that authorizes the possession of a weapon on private school property or in any school bus or vehicle used by a private school;

5. A gun, knife, bayonet, or other weapon in the possession of a member of a veterans group, the national guard, active military, the Reserve Officers' Training Corps (ROTC), or Junior ROTC, in order to participate in a ceremony, assembly, or educational program approved by the principal or chief administrator of a school or school district where the ceremony, assembly, or educational program is being held. The gun or other weapon that uses projectiles must be unloaded and inoperable at all times while on school property;
6. A handgun carried in a motor vehicle pursuant to a valid handgun license onto property set aside by a public or private elementary or secondary school for the use or parking of any vehicle. The handgun must be stored and hidden from view in a locked motor vehicle when the motor vehicle is left unattended on school property; and
7. A handgun carried onto public school property by school personnel who have been designated by the board of education. Such personnel must either:

   a. Possess a valid armed security guard license as

provided for in the Oklahoma Security Guard and Private Investigator Act, or

b. Hold a valid reserve peace officer certification as provided for by CLEET

if a policy has been adopted by the board of education of the school district that authorizes the carrying of a handgun onto public school property by such personnel. Nothing in this law restricts authority granted elsewhere in law to carry firearms.

"School property" means any publicly owned property held for purposes of elementary, secondary or vocational–technical education. It does not include property owned by public school districts or where such property is leased or rented to an individual or corporation and used for purposes other than educational. "Private school" means a school that offers a course of instruction for students in one or more grades from prekindergarten through grade twelve and is not operated by a governmental entity. "Motor vehicle" means any automobile, truck, minivan, or sports utility vehicle.

SOURCES: 21 O.S. § 1280.1, 70 O.S. § 3311, 37 O.S. 163.2, 37 O.S. 506, 21 O.S. § 99, 21 O.S. § 10, & Oklahoma Security Guard and Private Investigator Act

Parent Or Guardian Of Minor Child In Possession Of Firearm On School Property

Any custodial parent or guardian of a child under 18 years old whose child commits the crime of possession of a firearm on school property may be fined a maximum of $200, and/or ordered to perform a maximum of 40 hours of community service. To satisfy any community service requirement, the court may give preference to work that benefits the school their child attends. The penalty is an administrative penalty and will not be recorded on the custodial parent's or guardian's criminal record. Nothing in this law prohibits the filing or prosecution of any criminal charge.

SOURCE: 21 O.S. § 858

Carrying Firearms Where Liquor Is Consumed

It's a violation of 21 O.S. § 1272.1 to carry or possess any pistol, revolver, shotgun or rifle (whether loaded or unloaded), blackjack, loaded cane, billy, hand chain, metal knuckles, or any other offensive weapon in any establishment where low-point beer or alcoholic beverages are consumed. This doesn't apply to a peace officer, or to private investigators with a firearms authorization, when acting in the scope and course of employment. This also doesn't apply to an owner or proprietor of the establishment having a pistol, rifle, or shotgun on the premises. A person possessing a valid handgun license may carry the concealed or unconcealed handgun into any restaurant or other establishment licensed to dispense low-point beer or alcoholic beverages where the sale of low-point beer or alcoholic beverages does not constitute the primary purpose of the business.

Nothing in this law authorizes any peace officer in actual physical possession of a weapon to consume low-point beer or alcoholic beverages, except in the authorized line of duty as an undercover officer. Additionally, nothing in this law authorizes any private investigator with a firearms authorization in actual physical possession of a weapon to consume low-point beer or alcoholic beverages in any establishment where low-point beer or alcoholic beverages are consumed.

SOURCE: 21 O.S. § 1272.1

Carrying A Firearm In A Vehicle

The carrying of firearms in vehicles is covered in 21 O.S. § 1289.7. Anybody, except a convicted felon, may transport an open and unloaded rifle, shotgun, or pistol in a motor vehicle at any time. For purposes of this law, "open" means the firearm is transported in plain view, in a case (which must be wholly or partially visible) designed for carrying firearms, in a gun rack mounted in the vehicle, in an exterior locked compartment, or in a trunk of a vehicle.

Anybody, except a convicted felon, may transport in a motor vehicle a rifle or shotgun concealed behind a seat of the vehicle or within the interior of the vehicle—provided the rifle or shotgun is not clip, magazine, or chamber loaded.

SOURCE: 21 O.S. § 1289.7

Transporting A Loaded Firearm

Except as otherwise provided by the Oklahoma Self-Defense Act or another law, it's a violation of 21 O.S. § 1289.13 to transport a loaded pistol, rifle, or shotgun in a land-borne motor vehicle over a public highway or roadway. A rifle or shotgun may be transported clip or magazine loaded and not chamber loaded when transported in an exterior locked compartment of the vehicle, the trunk of the vehicle, or in the interior compartment of the vehicle when in possession of a valid handgun license.

This crime is a misdemeanor. The range of punishment in the county jail is 10 days–6 months. The range of fine is $50–$500.

Any person who is the operator of a vehicle or is a passenger in any vehicle wherein another person who is licensed to carry a handgun and is carrying a handgun or has a handgun, rifle, or shotgun in such vehicle will not be deemed in violation of this law so long as the licensee is in or near the vehicle.

SOURCES: 21 O.S. § 1289.13 & 21 O.S. § 1289.15

Improper Transportation Of Firearms

The improper transportation of firearms is a violation of 21 O.S. § 1289.13A. Any person stopped pursuant to a moving traffic violation who is transporting a loaded pistol in the motor vehicle without a valid handgun license authorized by the Oklahoma Self-Defense Act or valid license from another state, whether the loaded firearm is concealed or unconcealed in the vehicle, will be issued a $70 traffic citation and have to pay court costs. In addition to that traffic citation, the person may also be arrested for any other violation of law.

When the arresting officer determines that a valid handgun license exists for any person in the stopped vehicle, any firearms permitted to be carried pursuant to that license will not be confiscated, unless:

1. The person is arrested for violating a law other than a violation of this law. If the person is never charged with an offense pursuant to this paragraph, if the charges are dismissed, or the person is acquitted, then the weapon will be returned; or
2. The officer has probable cause to believe the weapon is:
   a. Contraband, or
   b. A firearm used in the commission of a crime other than transporting a loaded pistol in the motor vehicle without a valid handgun license while committing a moving violation.

Nothing in this law requires the confiscation of any

firearm.

SOURCE: 21 O.S. § 1289.13A

Prohibiting The Transportation And Storing Of Firearms Or Ammunition In A Locked Vehicle

It's a violation of 21 O.S. § 1289.7a for any person, property owner, tenant, employer, or business entity to maintain, establish, or enforce any policy or rule that has the effect of prohibiting any person, except a convicted felon, from transporting and storing firearms or ammunition in a locked motor vehicle or from transporting and storing firearms or ammunition locked in or locked to a motor vehicle on any property set aside for any motor vehicle.

No person, property owner, tenant, employer, or business entity is liable in any civil action for occurrences that result from the storing of firearms or ammunition in a locked motor vehicle on any property set aside for any motor vehicle, unless the person, property owner, tenant, employer, or owner of the business entity commits a criminal act involving the use of the firearms or ammunition.

An individual may bring a civil action to enforce this law. If the plaintiff prevails in a civil action related to the personnel manual against a person, property owner, tenant, employer, or business for a violation of this law, the court must award actual damages, enjoin further violations of this law, and award court costs and attorney fees to the prevailing plaintiff.

"Motor vehicle" means any automobile, truck, minivan, sports utility vehicle, motorcycle, motor scooter, and any other vehicle required to be registered under the Oklahoma Vehicle License and Registration Act.

SOURCE: 21 O.S. § 1289.7a

REQUIREMENTS FOR IDENTIFYING A GUN TO LAW ENFORCEMENT

It's a violation of 21 O.S. § 1290.8 to fail or refuse to identify the fact that you're in actual possession of a concealed or unconcealed handgun pursuant to the authority of the Oklahoma Self-Defense Act when you come into contact with any Oklahoma or federal law enforcement officer during the course of any arrest, detainment, or routine traffic stop. The identification to the law enforcement officer must be made at the first opportunity. You aren't required to identify yourself as a handgun licensee when no handgun is in your possession or in any vehicle in which you're driving or are a passenger.

A violation of this law is a misdemeanor. The maximum punishment in the county jail is one year. The maximum fine is $100.

If a law enforcement officer comes in contact with someone whose handgun license is suspended, revoked, or expired or someone who is in possession of a handgun license that has not been lawfully issued to that person, then the officer will confiscate the license.

SOURCES: 21 O.S. § 1290.8 & 21 O.S. § 10

Illegal Use Or Carrying Of Weapons

Crimes involving the illegal use or carrying of weapons in Oklahoma include Reckless Conduct; Unlawful Intent to Carry; Discharge Of Stun Gun, Tear Gas, Mace, Pepper Mace, or Other Deleterious Agent Against Officer; Use of Dangerous Weapon to Seize Bus or Assault or Batter a Bus Driver; Discharging Firearm or Hurling Missile at Bus; and Assault With Firearm Upon Emergency Medical Technician or Care Provider.

Reckless Conduct

It's a violation of 21 O.S. § 1289.11 to engage in reckless conduct while having in your possession any shotgun, rifle, or pistol. Reckless conduct consists of creating a situation of unreasonable risk and probability of death or great bodily harm to another and demonstrating a conscious disregard for the safety of another person.

A violation of this law is a misdemeanor. The range of punishment in the county jail is ten days–six months. The range of fine is $50–$500.

Anyone convicted of violating this law after having been issued a handgun license pursuant to the Oklahoma Self-Defense Act will have his or her license suspended for six months and will be subject to an administrative fine of $50. Prior to the suspension and fine, there must be a hearing and determination by the OSBI that the person violated this law.

SOURCES: 21 O.S. § 1289.11 & 21 O.S. § 1289.15

Unlawful Intent To Carry

It's a violation of 21 O.S. § 1278 to carry or wear any deadly weapon or dangerous instrument with the intent or for the avowed purpose of unlawfully injuring another person. The mere possession of such a weapon or dangerous instrument, without more, is not enough to establish the intent required by this law.

This crime is a felony. The maximum punishment in the Department of Corrections is two years. The maximum fine is $5,000.

Anyone convicted of violating this law after having been issued a handgun license pursuant to the Oklahoma Self-Defense Act will have their license permanently revoked and will be liable for an administrative fine of $1,000. There must first be a hearing and determination by the OSBI that the person violated this law.

SOURCE: 21 O.S. § 1278

Discharge Of Stun Gun, Tear Gas, Mace, Pepper Mace, Or Other Deleterious Agent Against Officer

It's a violation of 21 O.S. § 1272.3 to knowingly discharge, or cause to be discharged, any electrical stun gun, tear gas weapon, mace, tear gas, pepper mace, or any similar deleterious agent against another person knowing the other person is a peace officer, corrections officer, probation or parole officer, firefighter, emergency medical technician, or paramedic who is acting in the course of official duty.

This crime is a felony. The maximum punishment in the Department of Corrections is ten years. The maximum punishment in the county jail is one year.

SOURCE: 21 O.S. § 1272.3

Use Of Dangerous Weapon To Seize Bus Or Assault or Batter A Bus Driver

It's a violation of 21 O.S. § 1903 to seize or exercise control of any bus by force, violence, or threat of force or violence. This crime is a felony. The maximum punishment in the Department of Corrections is 20 years. The maximum fine is $20,000.

It's also a violation of 21 O.S. § 1903 to intimidate, threaten, assault or batter any driver, attendant, guard, or passenger of any bus with intent to seize or exercise control of any bus by force, violence, or threat of force or violence. The maximum punishment in the Department of Corrections is ten years. The maximum fine is $5,000.

These crimes are felonies. The maximum punishment in the Department of Corrections is 20 years. The maximum fine is $20,000.

SOURCE: 21 O.S. § 1903

Discharging Firearm Or Hurling Missile At Bus

It's a violation of 21 O.S. § 1903 to discharge any firearm into or within any bus, terminal, or other transportation facility, unless such action is determined to have been in defensive force resulting from reasonable fear of imminent peril of death or great bodily harm to oneself or another.

This crime is a felony. The maximum punishment in the Department of Corrections is five years. The maximum fine is $5,000.

SOURCE: 21 O.S. § 1903

Assault With Firearm Upon Emergency Medical Technician Or Care Provider

It's a violation of 21 O.S. § 650.5 to commit any aggravated assault and battery or any assault with a firearm or other deadly weapon upon an emergency medical technician or other emergency medical care provider without justifiable or excusable cause and with intent to do bodily harm.

This crime is a felony. The maximum punishment in the Department of Corrections is one year. The maximum fine is $1,000.

SOURCE: 21 O.S. § 650.5

PROHIBITED AMMUNITION

It's illegal to possess, use, manufacture, or load a handgun with restricted bullets. A "restricted bullet" is a round or elongated missile with a core of less than 60% lead and having a fluorocarbon coating that is designed to travel at a high velocity and is capable of penetrating body armor.

Prohibited Weapon

It's a violation of 21 O.S. § 1290.6 to carry any concealed or unconcealed handgun in a manner authorized by the Oklahoma Self-Defense Act when the handgun is loaded with any ammunition that is either a restricted bullet, is larger than .45 caliber, or is otherwise prohibited by law. Any weapon carried in this manner is deemed a prohibited weapon for purposes of the Oklahoma Self-Defense Act.

This crime is a misdemeanor. The maximum punishment in the county jail is 30 days. The range of fine for a first offense is $100–$250. On the second and subsequent violations, the range of punishment in the county jail is 30 days–3 months, and the range of fine is $250–$500.

In addition to any criminal prosecution for a violation of this law, the licensee will be subject to an administrative fine of $500. This occurs after a hearing and determination by the OSBI that the licensee violated this law.

SOURCES: 21 O.S. § 1290.6, 21 O.S § 1272, & 21 O.S § 1276

Possession Or Use Of Restricted Bullets

It's a violation of 21 O.S. § 1289.21 to possess, carry upon one's person, use, or attempt to use against another person any restricted bullet.

This crime is a felony. The range of punishment in the Department of Corrections is two–ten years. The sentence may not be suspended.

SOURCES: 21 O.S. § 1289.21 & 21 O.S. § 1289.19

Manufacture Of Restricted Bullets

It's a violation of 21 O.S. § 1289.20 to manufacture, cause to be manufactured, import, advertise for sale, or sell within Oklahoma any restricted bullet unless it's for the purpose of public safety or national security.

This crime is a felony. The maximum punishment in the Department of Corrections is ten years. The range of fine is $500–$10,000.

SOURCES: 21 O.S. § 1289.20 & 21 O.S. § 1289.19

Illegal Discharge Of Firearms

The illegal discharge of a firearm in Oklahoma can be either a misdemeanor or felony offense.

Misdemeanor Discharging Firearms

It's a violation of 21 O.S. § 1364 to willfully discharge any pistol, rifle, shotgun, air-gun, or other weapon, or throw any other missile in any public place, or in any place where there is any person to be endangered thereby—regardless of whether anyone is injured.

This crime is a misdemeanor. The maximum punishment in the county jail is one year. The maximum fine is $500.

Anyone convicted of violating this law after having been issued a handgun license pursuant to the Oklahoma Self-Defense Act will have their license suspended for six months and will be subject to an administrative fine of $50. This occurs after a hearing and determination by the OSBI that the person violated this law.

SOURCES: 21 O.S. § 1364 & 21 O.S. § 10

Felony Discharging Firearms

It's a violation of 21 O.S. § 1289.17A to willfully or intentionally discharge any firearm or other deadly weapon at or into any dwelling, or at or into any building used for public or business purposes.

This crime is a felony. The range of punishment in the Department of Corrections is 2–20 years. This law doesn't apply to law enforcement officers in the performance of any lawful duty.

SOURCE: 21 O.S. § 1289.17A

Removed Or Defaced Serial Number On Guns

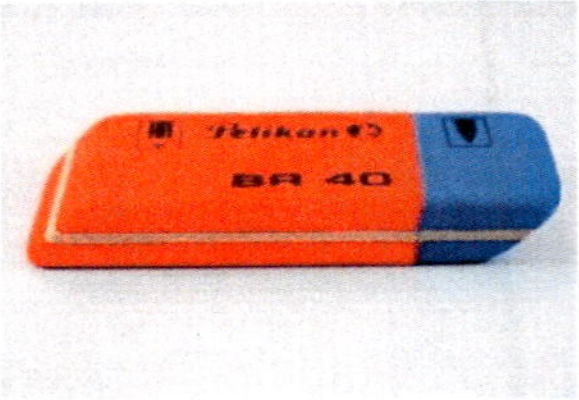

Removing or defacing the serial or identification number of a firearm is a misdemeanor. It's a felony to possess a firearm with a removed or defaced serial or identification number during the commission of a felony.

Upon a conviction of a violation of either of those laws, the court clerk, sheriff, peace officer, or other person having custody of the firearm must immediately deliver the firearm to the Commissioner of Public Safety, who will preserve the firearm pending an order of the court. If a finding is made at the conclusion of a trial or proceeding for a violation of this law that the factory serial number or identification number of the firearm has been removed, defaced, altered, obliterated, or mutilated, then the court must issue a written order to the Commissioner of Public Safety for destruction of the firearm—unless the defendant files a timely motion to preserve the firearm pending appeal. If a finding is made at the conclusion of the appeal that the factory serial number or identification number of the firearm has been removed, defaced, altered, obliterated, or mutilated, then the Court of Criminal Appeals or the trial court must issue a written order to the Commissioner for destruction of the firearm.

Removing Or Defacing The Serial Or Identification Number Of A Firearm

It's a violation of 21 O.S. § 1550 to remove, deface, alter, obliterate, or mutilate the factory serial number or identification number of a firearm, or participate in that activity.

This crime is a misdemeanor. The maximum punishment in the county jail is one year. The maximum fine is $1,000.

SOURCE: 21 O.S. § 1550

Possessing Firearm With Removed Or Defaced Serial Or Identification Number During The Commission Of A Felony

It's a violation of 21 O.S. § 1550 to possess or control a firearm that's had its factory serial number or identification number removed, defaced, altered, obliterated, or mutilated in any manner while in the commission or attempted commission of a felony.

This crime is a felony. The range of punishment in the Department of Corrections is two–five years. The range of fine is $1,000–$10,000.

SOURCE: 21 O.S. § 1550

POSSESSION OF SAWED-OFF SHOTGUN OR SAWED-OFF RIFLE

It's a violation of 21 O.S. § 1289.18 to have a sawed-off shotgun or a sawed-off rifle in your possession or under your immediate control, whether its concealed or not.

This crime is a felony. The maximum punishment in the Department of Corrections is two years. The maximum fine is $1,000.

It is a defense to prosecution under this law to introduce the approved application form that authorized the making or transfer of the particular firearm to the defendant. The form must indicate that the registration of the firearm to the defendant is pursuant to the National Firearms Act.

A "sawed-off shotgun" is any firearm capable of discharging a series of projectiles of any material that may reasonably be expected to be able to cause lethal injury. The barrel or barrels must be less than 18" long. It must use either gunpowder, gas, or any means of rocket propulsion.

A "sawed-off rifle" is any rifle having a barrel or barrels of less than 16" long or any weapon made from a rifle (whether by alteration, modification, or otherwise) if such a weapon, as modified, has an overall length of less than 26" long, including the stock portion.

SOURCE: 21 O.S. § 1289.18

USE OF BODY ARMOR

It's a violation of 21 O.S. § 1289.26 to commit or attempt to commit a felony while wearing body armor. This will be a separate offense from the felony committed or attempted.

This crime is a felony. The maximum punishment in the Department of Corrections for the first offense is three years. The maximum punishment in the Department of Corrections for the second offense is ten years. The maximum punishment in the Department of Corrections for the third and subsequent offenses is 20 years.

"Body armor" means a vest or shirt of ten plies or more of bullet resistant material as defined by the Office of Development, Testing and Dissemination, a division of the United States Department of Justice.

SOURCES: 21 O.S. § 1289.26 & 21 O.S. § 1289.19

Teaching, Demonstrating, Or Training In The Use Of Firearms, Explosives, Or Incendiary Devices In Furtherance Of Riot Or Civil Disorder

It's a violation of 21 O.S. § 1320.10 for someone, other than those specifically authorized by the state or federal government, to:

1. Teach or demonstrate to any group of people the use, application, or making of any firearm, explosive, or incendiary device or application of physical force capable of causing injury or death to a person knowing or intending that such firearm, explosive, or incendiary device or application of physical force will be employed for use in, or in furtherance of, a riot or civil disorder; or

2. Assemble with one or more people for the purpose of training with, practicing with, or being instructed in the use of any firearm, explosive, or incendiary device or application of physical force capable of causing injury or death to a person, intending to employ such firearm, explosive, or incendiary device or application of physical force for use in, or in furtherance of, a riot

or civil disorder.

This crime is a felony. The maximum punishment in the Department of Corrections is two years. The maximum fine is $1,000.

SOURCE: 21 O.S. § 1320.10 & 21 O.S. § 9

WHAT ARE 85 PERCENT CRIMES AND HOW DO THEY RELATE TO GUN CRIMES?

Oklahoma refers to some crimes as "85% crimes." These crimes are listed in 21 O.S. § 13.1. They are considered the worst types of crimes that can be committed. Individuals convicted of these crimes are not eligible to earn any credits that have the effect of reducing the length of the sentence to less than 85% of the sentence imposed.

85% crimes that could involve firearms:

1. Murder (21 O.S. §§ 701.7 & 701.8);
2. Manslaughter in the first degree (21 O.S. § 711);
3. Rape in the first degree (21 O.S. § 1114);
4. Shooting with intent to kill (21 O.S. § 652);
5. Drive-by shooting (21 O.S. § 652);
6. Assault and battery with a deadly weapon or by other means likely to produce death or great bodily harm (21 O.S. § 652); and
7. Robbery with a dangerous weapon (21 O.S. § 801).

SOURCE: 21 O.S. § 13.1

How Does The Use Of A Gun Affect A Charge In Oklahoma?

In general, the use of a gun will turn a crime that might have otherwise been a nonviolent crime into a violent crime. The primary effect of that will be to increase the time the defendant may spend in prison. It can also increase the mandatory minimum amount of time the defendant will have to spend in prison.

Enhancement For Weapon Possession

Anyone who discharges a firearm while committing or attempting to commit a crime of violence, in addition to the penalty provided by statute for the crime of violence committed or attempted, upon conviction, may be charged with an additional felony for possessing such weapon. The district attorney has discretion to charge this additional crime. This separate offense is a felony.

The minimum punishment in the Department of Corrections is ten years. This time may be served concurrently with the sentence for the crime of violence.

"Crime of violence" means an offense that is a felony and has as an element of the offense, the use, attempted use, or threatened use of physical force against someone or that by its nature involves a substantial risk that physical force against someone may be used in the course of committing the offense. "Firearm" means a rifle, pistol, or shotgun.

SOURCE: 21 O.S. § 1287.1

Violent Crimes In Oklahoma

Oklahoma considers some crimes "violent" crimes. These are listed in 57 O.S. § 571. A defendant convicted of a violent crime must serve a greater percentage of their sentence before being eligible for parole.

Violent crimes that could involve firearms:

1. Murder (21 O.S. §§ 701.7 & 701.8);
2. Manslaughter (21 O.S. §§ 711 & 716);
3. Rape in the first degree (21 O.S. § 1114);
4. Assault, battery, or assault and battery with a dangerous or deadly weapon (21 O.S. § 652);
5. Shooting with intent to kill (21 O.S. § 652);
6. Assault, battery, or assault and battery with a deadly weapon or by other means likely to produce death or

great bodily harm (21 O.S. § 652);

7. Armed robbery (21 O.S. § 801);
8. Robbery with dangerous weapon or imitation firearm (21 O.S. § 801);
9. Use of a firearm or offensive weapon to commit or attempt to commit a felony (921 O.S. § 1287);
10. Drive-by shooting (21 O.S. § 652); and
11. Pointing firearms (21 O.S. § 1289.16).

SOURCE: 57 O.S. § 571

"Unborn child" means the unborn offspring of human beings from the moment of conception, through pregnancy, and until live birth including the human conceptus, zygote, morula, blastocyst, embryo, and fetus.

The laws on Shooting With Intent to Kill, Assault and Battery with a Deadly Weapon, and Drive-By Shooting don't apply to:

1. Acts that cause the death of an unborn child if those acts were committed during a legal abortion to which the pregnant woman consented; or
2. Acts that are committed pursuant to usual and customary standards of medical practice during diagnostic testing or therapeutic treatment.

Under no circumstances will the mother of the unborn child be prosecuted for causing the death of the unborn child unless the mother has committed a crime that caused the death of the unborn child.

Assault And Battery With A Deadly Weapon

It's a violation of 21 O.S. § 652 to commit any assault and battery upon another, including an unborn child, by means of any deadly weapon, or by such other means or force as is likely to produce death, or in any manner attempt to kill another, including an unborn child, or in resisting the execution of any legal process. The maximum punishment in the Department of Corrections is life.

SOURCES: 21 O.S. § 652 & 63 O.S. § 1-730

Shooting With Intent To Kill

It's a violation of 21 O.S. § 652 to intentionally and wrongfully shoot another with, or discharge, any kind of firearm, with intent to kill any person, including an unborn child. This crime is a felony. The maximum punishment in the Department of Corrections is life.

SOURCES: 21 O.S. § 652 & 63 O.S. § 1-730

Drive-By Shooting

It's a violation of 21 O.S. § 652 to use a vehicle to facilitate the intentional discharge of any kind of firearm, crossbow, or other weapon in conscious disregard for the safety of any other person, including an unborn child. This crime is a felony. The range of punishment in the Department of Corrections is two years–life.

SOURCES: 21 O.S. § 652 & 63 O.S. § 1-730

Robbery Or Attempted Robbery With Dangerous Weapon Or Imitation Firearm

It's a violation of 21 O.S. § 801 to use any firearms or any other dangerous weapons (whether the firearm is loaded or not) or use a blank or imitation firearm (which is capable of raising in the mind of the one threatened with such device a fear that it is a real firearm) to rob or attempt to rob someone or rob or attempt to rob any place of business, residence, banking institution, or any other place inhabited or attended by someone at any time.

This crime is a felony. The range of punishment in the Department of Corrections is five years–life. Upon conviction of this crime, any person guilty of three separate and distinct felonies, in violation of this law, must be punished by a minimum of ten years in the Department of Corrections. The ten-year minimum sentence is mandatory. The sentence imposed upon such person can neither be reduced to less than ten calendar years nor suspended. No person may be eligible for probation or parole or receive any deduction from his or her sentence for good conduct until he or she has served ten calendar years of such sentence.

A dangerous weapon is any instrument that's likely to produce death or great bodily harm in the manner it is used or attempted to be used. A deadly weapon is an instrument designed or constructed to cause death or great bodily injury. A pistol, revolver, dagger, bowie, dirk, switch-blade, spring-type knife, sword cane, knife having a blade that opens automatically, blackjack, loaded cane, billy, metal knuckles, and hand chain is a deadly weapon.
SOURCE: 21 O.S. § 801 & OUJI-CR 4-28

Use of Firearm While Committing a Felony

It's a violation of 21 O.S. § 1287 for any person to commit or attempt to commit a felony while possessing a(n):

- Pistol, shotgun, rifle, or any other offensive weapon in such commission or attempt, whether the pistol, shotgun, or rifle is loaded or not;

- Blank or imitation pistol, altered air or toy pistol, shotgun, or rifle capable of raising in the mind of one threatened with such device a fear that it is a real pistol, shotgun, or rifle;
- Air gun or carbon dioxide or other gas-filled weapon;
- Electronic dart gun;
- Conductive energy weapon;
- Knife;
- Dagger;
- Dirk;
- Switchblade knife;
- Blackjack;
- Ax;
- Loaded cane;
- Billy;
- Hand chain; or
- Metal knuckles.

This will be a separate felony from the felony committed or attempted. The range of punishment in the Department of Corrections is two–ten years for a first offense. The range of punishment in the Department of Corrections for a second or subsequent offense is 10–30 years.

Anyone convicted of violating this law after having been issued a handgun license pursuant to the Oklahoma Self-Defense Act will have their license permanently revoked and will be liable for an administrative fine of $1,000. There must first be a hearing and determination by the OSBI that the person violated this law.

"Altered toy pistol" means any toy weapon that has been altered from its original manufactured state to resemble a real weapon.

"Altered air pistol" means any air pistol manufactured to propel projectiles by air pressure that has been altered from its original manufactured state.

SOURCE: 21 O.S. § 1287

Pointing Firearms

Except for an act of self-defense, it's a violation of 21 O.S. § 1289.16 to willfully or without lawful cause point a shotgun, rifle, pistol, or any deadly weapon (whether loaded or not) at anyone for the purpose of threatening, with the intention of discharging the firearm, with any malice, or for any purpose of injuring someone. The injury must be either through physical injury or mental or emotional intimidation or for purposes of whimsy, humor, or prank, or in anger or otherwise. This doesn't include the pointing of shotguns, rifles, or pistols by: law enforcement authorities in the performance of their duties; armed security guards licensed by the Council on Law Enforcement Education and Training pursuant to the Oklahoma Security Guard and Private Investigator Act in the performance of their duties; members of the state military forces in the performance of their duties; members of the federal military reserve and active military components in the performance of their duties; any federal government law enforcement officer in the performance of any duty; actors performing a play on stage, rodeo, television, or on film; someone defending any person; or someone defending their home or property.

This crime is a felony. The range of punishment in the Department of Corrections is one–ten years.

Anyone who violates this law after having been issued a handgun license pursuant to the Oklahoma Self-Defense Act will have their license revoked and will be subject to an administrative fine of $1,000. There must first be a hearing and determination by the OSBI that the person violated this law.

“Defensive force" includes, but is not limited to, pointing a weapon at a perpetrator in self-defense or in order to thwart, stop, or deter a forcible felony or attempted forcible felony.

SOURCES: 21 O.S. § 1289.16, 21 O.S. § 1289.25, & 21 O.S. § 1289.17

Pointing Weapons at Others

Except for an act of self-defense, it’s a violation of 21 O.S. § 1279 to point any pistol or any other deadly weapon (whether loaded or not) at somebody. This law differs from Pointing Firearms in that this law does not require a mental state. The act of pointing a firearm, alone, is sufficient to violate this law.

This crime is a misdemeanor, so it is not considered a “violent crime” in Oklahoma. The range of fine is $100–$1,000. The range of punishment in the county jail is 3–12 months.

Someone convicted of this crime after having been issued a handgun license pursuant to the Oklahoma Self-Defense

Act will have their handgun license permanently revoked and will be liable for an administrative fine of $50. There must first be a hearing and determination by the OSBI that the person violated this law.

SOURCES: 21 O.S. § 1279 & 21 O.S. § 1280

What Defenses Can Be Used In Gun Charge Cases?

The primary defense that can be used when there is a crime involving the discharge of a firearm is self-defense. Oklahoma recognizes the right to defend oneself against violence. The first thing that must be looked at when facing a charge involving the discharge of a firearm is who the instigator was. If the defendant shot someone in self-defense, then the defendant has a good defense to a charge involving the unlawful use of the firearm.

Some gun charges make the possession of a firearm illegal under certain circumstances. A strong defense to these crimes is that the defendant did not have possession of the firearm. This would mean the defendant had neither actual nor physical control. The defendant cannot have been in joint control of the firearm with someone else. To prove possession, the defendant must have had knowledge of the firearm and the ability to control the disposition of it.

Other defenses to gun charges include:

- Someone else did it
- Not enough evidence
- Didn't meet all the elements of the offense
- Intoxicated
- No intent (where required)
- Not a firearm

Prosecutors look very unfavorably on gun crimes. The belief is that the use of a firearm adds an entirely new level of danger to a situation. Therefore, prosecutors are generally less inclined to be lenient in plea negotiations for gun crimes. Additionally, prosecutors typically have a very harsh stance on felons in possession of a firearm. It won't matter what the original felony was. The thought from the prosecutor's perspective is that the felon's gun rights were taken away for a reason, and a felon's disregard of that law makes that felon a greater danger to society. Some prosecutors require minimum prison time for felons caught in possession of a firearm—regardless of the reason the individual became a felon and regardless of circumstances surrounding the new incident. Unfortunately, this mentality is one of the reasons Oklahoma's prisons are overflowing. Maybe the felon lived in a bad neighborhood and needed the gun for protection. Or, maybe the felon was using the gun in self-defense. Nevertheless, prosecutors take offenses involving firearms very seriously. That's why it's important to hire a lawyer who understands the stakes involved in a firearm charge and who has experience defending offenses involving firearms.

WHAT'S OKLAHOMA'S SELF-DEFENSE LAW?

Oklahoma citizens have a right to expect absolute safety within their own homes or places of business.

Any person or owner, manager, or employee of a business is presumed to have held a reasonable fear of imminent peril of death or great bodily harm to himself, herself, or another when using defensive force that is intended or likely to cause death or great bodily harm to another if:

1. The person against whom the defensive force was used was in the process of unlawfully and forcefully entering, or had unlawfully and forcibly entered, a dwelling, residence, occupied vehicle, or place of business, or if that person had removed or was attempting to remove another against the will of that person from the dwelling, residence, occupied vehicle, or place of business; and
2. The person who uses defensive force knew or had reason to believe that an unlawful and forcible entry or unlawful and forcible act was occurring or had occurred.

The above presumption doesn't apply if:

1. The person against whom the defensive force is used has the right to be in or is a lawful resident of the dwelling, residence, or vehicle. Examples include an owner, lessee, or titleholder. There can't be a protective order from domestic violence in effect or a written pretrial supervision order of no contact against that person;
2. The person or persons sought to be removed are children or grandchildren or are otherwise in the lawful custody or under the lawful guardianship of the person against whom the defensive force is used; or
3. The person who uses defensive force is engaged in an unlawful activity or is using the dwelling, residence, occupied vehicle, or place of business to further an unlawful activity.

A person who is not engaged in an unlawful activity and who is attacked in any other place where he or she has a right to be has no duty to retreat and has the right to stand his or her ground and meet force with force, including deadly force, if he or she reasonably believes it's necessary to do so to prevent death or great bodily harm to himself, herself, or another or to prevent the commission of a forcible felony. This is Oklahoma's "Stand Your Ground" law.

A person who unlawfully and by force enters or attempts to enter the dwelling, residence, occupied vehicle of another person, or a place of business is presumed to be doing so with the intent to commit an unlawful act involving force or violence. A person who uses defensive force, as permitted pursuant to the above paragraphs, is justified in using such defensive force and is immune from criminal prosecution and civil action for the use of such defensive force. This is known as the "Castle Doctrine."

A law enforcement agency may use standard procedures for investigating the use of defensive force, but the law enforcement agency may not arrest the person for using defensive force unless it determines that there is probable cause that the defensive force that was used was unlawful. A court will award reasonable attorney fees, court costs, compensation for loss of income, and all expenses incurred by the defendant in defense of any civil action brought by a plaintiff if the court finds that the defendant is immune from prosecution as provided in this law.

This law and the Oklahoma Self-Defense Act may not be construed to require any person using a weapon in accordance with this law to be licensed in any manner. Someone who points a weapon at a perpetrator in self-defense or in order to thwart, stop, or deter a forcible felony or attempted forcible felony may not be deemed guilty of committing a criminal act.

“Criminal prosecution" includes charging or prosecuting the defendant.

"Defensive force" includes, but is not limited to, pointing a weapon at a perpetrator in self-defense or to thwart, stop, or deter a forcible felony or attempted forcible felony.

"Dwelling" means a building or conveyance of any kind, including any attached porch, whether the building or conveyance is temporary or permanent, mobile or immobile, which has a roof over it, including a tent, and is designed to be occupied by people.

"Residence" means a dwelling in which a person resides either temporarily or permanently or is visiting as an invited guest.

"Vehicle" means a conveyance of any kind, whether or not motorized, which is designed to transport people or property.

SOURCE: 21 O.S. § 1289.25

How Do I Apply For A Handgun License In Oklahoma?

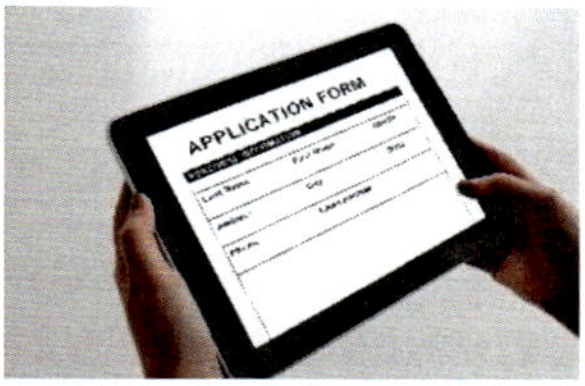

Applications for a handgun license are available from the county sheriff or by mail from the OSBI. The application must be made under oath and signed in person before the sheriff of the county where applicant resides. Along with the application, you must submit $100, two passport-sized photographs, and the original certificate of training or exemption certificate. The $100 fee is for a five-year license. You may also get a ten-year license for $200. The cost to renew a license is lower than the cost of an initial application.

You must show a valid photo ID. The sheriff will take two complete sets of fingerprints. The charge for these will be no more than $25. The sheriff will make a preliminary investigation and submit the application with any relevant information to the OSBI within 14 days. The OSBI will conduct a state and federal criminal background search, a federal fingerprint search, and any other relevant checks before issuing a license or denying the application within 90 days of receipt of the application. The OSBI will deny a license when the applicant fails to properly complete the application form or application process or is determined ineligible as specified in the Oklahoma Self-Defense Act. You have 60 days to appeal a denial. Application materials remain available to law enforcement personnel for law enforcement purposes only.

The qualifying firearm safety and training course may be taken from a firearms instructor who is approved and registered in the state or from an interactive online firearms safety and training course that's approved and certified by CLEET. You're also required to demonstrate competency and qualification. The course and the demonstration of competency and qualification must be designed as one that an applicant can reasonably complete in eight hours. It can't cost more than $60.

Authorization for any type of pistol requires training and demonstration of competency under an approved firearms instructor. The course provides an opportunity for the applicant to qualify himself or herself on either a derringer, a revolver, a semiautomatic pistol, or any combination of those three types of guns. A pistol can't be capable of firing larger than .45 caliber ammunition. The firearm instructor will refuse to train or qualify anyone whose handgun is unauthorized, deemed unsafe, or unfit for firing. An applicant who successfully trains and qualifies with a semiautomatic pistol may be approved by the firearms instructor on the training certificate for a semiautomatic pistol, a revolver, and a derringer upon request of the applicant. Someone who qualifies on a derringer or revolver is not eligible for a semiautomatic rating until he or she demonstrates competence and qualifications on a semiautomatic pistol. Applicants who successfully complete the training and qualification course receive a certificate of training and a certificate of competency and qualification.

SOURCES: 21 O.S. § 1290.12, 21 O.S. § 1290.13, 21 O.S. § 1290.5, & 21 O.S. § 1290.14

A firearms charge can be devastating to a military career. In my over 19 years in the military, I have seen careers ended due to just being charged with a crime. If you get arrested for a crime, your career could effectively be over. You typically won't be allowed to promote or re-enlist. If you are ever charged with any firearms offense, then your odds of getting into the military are slim to none.

An issue that I see with members of the military, having been on active-duty for over ten years, is that members who get arrested are believed to be guilty just because they were arrested. Our system is supposed to presume people innocent until proven guilty. Unfortunately, that's not the case with many military unit commanders. What they typically do is try to make an example out of people.

Take an arrest that happens over the weekend as an example. The commander will find out about it and have the individual report in their service dress uniform early Monday morning. The commander will grill them about what happened. The member may even have to talk to several commanders about what happened. Additionally, the individual may have to stand before his or her peers and explain what happened. I've even seen a situation where the commander opened it up to questions from members of the audience. People in the audience were asking the arrestee questions! So, these are all things that members of the military can be subjected to—shame, embarrassment, and railroading.

The biggest problem here is the breakdown in the presumption of innocence. Therefore, I try as hard as I can to get across the importance of maintaining the presumption of innocence. If you go before your commander, then you can exercise your right to remain silent. You don't have to tell people what happened. What you say can and will be held against you—even though it's not to law enforcement. Once you tell one person, it's over. Let your attorney look over the evidence and discuss your case with you before you talk about it with anybody. You'll be threatened and made to feel bad, but just know that you have rights. Don't let higher-ranking people trample on those rights.

If you're in the military and you get arrested, you can be tried on or off base. If it's off base, then it will be handled by the state or city prosecutor. It's usually not transferred to the JAG office on base. However, that does happen sometimes. If you're arrested on base, then it's possible that your case will be prosecuted on base. The base's Area Defense Counsel (ADC) helps defend people on base. They're the public defenders for members of the military. You can certainly hire a private attorney to handle your case on base. You would want somebody who's familiar with the UCMJ, the Uniform Code of Military Justice, because that's the body of law that they'll be using to prosecute you.

If you're prosecuted off base, you want representation from someone who's familiar with the procedures and the law for whatever jurisdiction is prosecuting you. Therefore, the ADC will likely not be helping you if your case is prosecuted off base.

Another consequence that arrested members of the military face is an Article 15—known as "non-judicial punishment." Instead of going through a Court Martial, the commander can punish the member through an Article 15. This basically means that the commander can punish the member in some way. Instead of going through a Court Martial, they put pressure on the members to talk and implicate themselves. It's difficult to get out of it at that point.

The Article 15 is often the easiest way for the commander to go. The punishments can range from extra duty on the weekends to being confined to base—or even to getting kicked out. What often happens after a service member's arrest is that the punishment received through an Article 15 is something that makes the service member un-promotable, so they must separate when their time is up. The punishment varies based on the severity of the crime that the member is alleged to have committed.

When a soldier is accused of breaking the law, the Army issues a General Officer Memorandum of Reprimand (GOMOR). This is written by a General Officer reprimanding a soldier for their alleged bad behavior. The GOMOR can become part of the soldier's military files. If it's filed locally, then it will eventually be removed from the soldier's files. A GOMOR filed in the soldier's permanent file will likely stay there forever; this is devastating to a soldier's chances of staying in the Army. It's important for a soldier to do whatever is necessary to prevent the GOMOR from becoming a permanent part of his or her file.

If you had planned on making the military a career, then one lapse in judgment can end those dreams. So, it's very important to hire an attorney who understands what's going on with the military, the culture there, and what they're going to try to do to you. You must find an attorney who is going to do everything they can to obtain an outcome that's not going to end your career.

Business Owner Gun Rights

The statute that outlines business owner rights regarding concealed and unconcealed firearms is 21 O.S. § 1290.22. A person, property owner, tenant, employer, holder of an event permit, place of worship, or business entity that doesn't prohibit the carrying of a concealed or unconcealed weapon is immune from liability arising from the carrying of a concealed or unconcealed weapon. The incident must occur while in the scope of employment. The incident must either happen on the property or in or about a business entity vehicle.

Except as provided in 21 O.S. § 1290.22 subsections B, C, and D, nothing contained in any provision of the Oklahoma Self-Defense Act will limit, restrict, or prohibit in any manner the existing rights of any person, property owner, tenant, employer, place of worship, or business entity to control the possession of weapons on any property owned or controlled by the person or business entity.

Firearms in Parking Lots of Businesses

No person, property owner, tenant, employer, holder of an event permit, place of worship, or business entity may establish any policy or rule that has the effect of prohibiting any person, except a convicted felon, from transporting and storing firearms in a locked vehicle on any property set aside for any vehicle.

Prohibiting Firearms on Business Property

A property owner, tenant, employer, place of worship, or business entity may prohibit any person from carrying a concealed or unconcealed firearm on the property. If the building or property is open to the public, the property owner, tenant, employer, place of worship, or business entity must post signs on or about the property stating the prohibition.

The carrying of a concealed or unconcealed firearm by someone who has been issued a handgun license on property that has signs prohibiting the carrying of firearms is not a criminal act. You may be denied entrance onto the property or removed from the property. If you refuse to leave the property and a peace officer is summoned, you may be issued a citation of no more than $250.

No person, property owner, tenant, employer, holder of an event permit, place of worship, or business entity may establish any policy or rule that has the effect of prohibiting any person from carrying a concealed or unconcealed firearm on property within the specific exclusion of any property designated by a city, town, county, or state governmental authority as a park, recreational area, or fairgrounds; provided that carrying a concealed or unconcealed firearm may be prohibited in the following places:

1. The portion of a public property structure or building during an event authorized by the city, town, county, state, or federal governmental authority owning or controlling such building or structure;
2. Any public property sports field, including any adjacent seating or adjacent area set aside for viewing a sporting event, where an elementary or secondary school, collegiate, or professional sporting event or an International Olympic Committee or organization or any committee subordinate to the International Olympic Committee event is being held;
3. The fairgrounds during the Oklahoma State Fair or the Tulsa State Fair; and
4. The portion of a public property structure or building that is leased or under contract to a business or not-for-profit entity or group for offices.

Business Owner Liability

Any person, property owner, tenant, employer, holder of an event permit, place of worship, or business entity is immune from any liability despite their decision to prohibit or not prohibit any individual except a convicted felon from carrying a loaded or unloaded, concealed or unconcealed weapon on property they own or have legal control of. Except for acts of gross negligence or willful or malicious misconduct, an employer who does or does not prohibit their employees from carrying a concealed or unconcealed weapon is immune from any liability arising from that decision. A person, property owner, tenant, employer, holder of an event permit, place of worship, or business entity that does not prohibit persons from carrying a concealed or unconcealed weapon in accordance with the law is immune from any liability arising from the carrying of a concealed or unconcealed weapon, while in the scope of employment, on the property, or in or about a business entity vehicle.

It's not considered part of an employee's job description or within the employee's scope of employment if an employee is allowed to carry or discharge a weapon pursuant to this section. Nothing in this law can prevent an employer, employee or person who has suffered loss resulting from the discharge of a weapon to seek redress or damages of the person who discharged the weapon or used the weapon outside the provisions of the Oklahoma Self-Defense Act.

SOURCE: 21 O.S. § 1290.22

Domestic Violence Charges & Firearms

It's a federal crime to possess a firearm after being convicted of a misdemeanor crime of domestic violence. It's illegal to possess a firearm after any felony conviction—including a felony domestic violence crime.

The federal Domestic Violence Offender Gun ban is often referred to as the "Lautenberg Amendment." It prohibits the shipment, transport, and possession of guns or ammunition by individuals convicted of a misdemeanor crime of domestic violence or who are subject to a victim protective order. The Lautenberg Amendment also makes it illegal to knowingly sell or give a firearm or ammunition to such persons.

The victim protective order ban applies to people restrained from harassing, stalking, or threatening an intimate partner of the person or the child of an intimate partner or person or engaging in other conduct that would place an intimate partner in reasonable fear of bodily injury to the partner or child. An "intimate partner" is, with respect to a person, the spouse of the person, a former spouse of the person, an individual who is a parent of a child of the person, and an individual who cohabitates or has cohabited with the person.

A "misdemeanor crime of domestic violence" is an offense that:

A. is a misdemeanor under Federal, State, or Tribal law; and
B. has, as an element, the use or attempted use of physical force, or the threatened use of a deadly weapon, committed by a current or former spouse, parent, or guardian of the victim, by a person with whom the victim shares a child in common, by a person who is cohabiting with or has cohabited with the victim as a spouse, parent, or guardian; or by a person similarly situated to a spouse, parent, or guardian of the victim.

A person is not considered to have been convicted of a misdemeanor crime of domestic violence, unless:

A. the person was represented by counsel in the case, or knowingly and intelligently waived the right to counsel in the case; and
B. in the case of a prosecution for an offense for which a person was entitled to a jury trial in the jurisdiction in which the case was tried, either

a. the case was tried by a jury, or
b. the person knowingly and intelligently waived the right to have the case tried by a jury, by guilty plea or otherwise.

A person is not considered to have been convicted of a misdemeanor crime of domestic violence if the conviction has been expunged or set aside, or is an offense for which the person has been pardoned or has had civil rights restored (if the law of the applicable jurisdiction provides for the loss of civil rights under such an offense) unless the pardon, expungement, or restoration of civil rights expressly provides that the person may not ship, transport, possess, or receive firearms.

SOURCES: 18 U.S.C. § 921 & 18 U.S.C. § 922

Handgun License Reciprocity With Other States

Oklahoma recognizes any valid concealed or unconcealed carry weapons permit, valid military identification cards, and valid licenses issued by another state. If the state is a nonpermitting carry state, Oklahoma will reciprocate under the permitting law of that state.

Anyone entering Oklahoma in possession of a firearm authorized for concealed or unconcealed carry upon the authority and license of another state or a valid military identification card is authorized to continue to carry a concealed or unconcealed firearm and license in Oklahoma. The license from the other state or valid military identification card must be valid. The firearm must either be carried unconcealed or concealed. Upon coming in contact with any Oklahoma peace officer, the person must disclose the fact that he or she is in possession of a concealed or unconcealed firearm pursuant to a valid concealed or unconcealed carry weapons permit, license, or a valid military identification card issued in another state.

Constitutional Carry States

Anyone entering Oklahoma in possession of a firearm authorized for concealed carry upon the authority of a state that is a nonpermitted carry state and the person is in compliance with the Oklahoma Self-Defense Act, the person is authorized to carry a concealed or unconcealed firearm in this state. A nonpermitting state is one that permits the carrying of a handgun, either openly or concealed, without a license or permit. This is sometimes referred to as "constitutional carry," "permitless carry," or "unrestricted carry." In 2018, Oklahoma's governor vetoed a bill that would have made Oklahoma a constitutional carry state.

The firearm must be either carried fully concealed or unconcealed. Upon coming in contact with an Oklahoma peace officer, you must disclose the fact that you're in possession of a concealed or unconcealed firearm pursuant to the nonpermitting laws of the state in which you're a legal resident. You must present proper identification by a valid photo ID as proof that you're a legal resident in such a nonpermitting state.

Anyone who is 21 years old or older having a valid firearm license from another state may apply for a handgun license in Oklahoma immediately upon establishing a residence in Oklahoma.

According to the OSBI, the following states honor Oklahoma's handgun licenses: Alaska, Alabama, Arkansas, Arizona, Colorado, Delaware, Florida, Georgia, Idaho, Indiana, Iowa, Kansas, Kentucky, Louisiana, Maine, Michigan, Mississippi, Missouri, Montana, Nebraska, Nevada, New Hampshire, New Mexico, North Carolina, North Dakota, Ohio, Pennsylvania, South Carolina, South Dakota, Tennessee, Texas, Utah, Vermont, Virginia, Washington, West Virginia, & Wyoming.

According to the OSBI, the following states do not honor Oklahoma's handgun licenses: California, Connecticut, Hawaii, Illinois, Maryland, Massachusetts, Minnesota, New Jersey, New York, Oregon, Rhode Island, Washington D.C., & Wisconsin.

SOURCES: 21 O.S. § 1290.26, Oklahoma Self-Defense Act Reciprocity

Can I Have A Gun If I Have A Medical Marijuana License In Oklahoma?

On June 26, 2018, voters in Oklahoma overwhelmingly approved medical marijuana by approving SQ 788. The legality of having a gun while possessing a medical marijuana license became a hot topic immediately after the vote. According to federal law, it's illegal to possess a gun if you are a medical marijuana license holder—regardless of state law.

The federal law that controls this issue is 18 U.S.C. § 922. Subsection (g) states that it's unlawful for "any person who is an unlawful user of or addicted to any controlled substance (as defined in section 102 of the Controlled Substances Act (21 U.S.C. 802) . . . to ship or transport in interstate or foreign commerce, or possess in or affecting commerce, any firearm or ammunition; or to receive any firearm or ammunition which has been shipped or transported in interstate or foreign commerce." Succinctly, anyone who illegally uses any drug defined as a controlled substance by the federal government cannot possess a gun. Marijuana is a Schedule I substance on the federal schedule, so the federal government considers every user of marijuana an illegal user of a controlled substance. And possessing a state license for medical marijuana doesn't make somebody a legal marijuana user in the eyes of the federal government. Note that you don't have to be an addict for this statute to apply—merely a user.

Possessing a gun or ammunition as a user of illegal drugs is a felony. The maximum punishment in federal prison is ten years.

Furthermore, it's illegal "for any person to sell or otherwise dispose of any firearm or ammunition to any person knowing or having reasonable cause to believe that such person . . . is an unlawful user of or addicted to any controlled substance (as defined in section 102 of the Controlled Substances Act (21 U.S.C. 802))." Succinctly, it's illegal to sell or transfer a gun to someone you reasonably believe is an illegal drug user. What could give someone the reasonable belief that you're an illegal drug user? A medical marijuana license! The Bureau of Alcohol, Tobacco, Firearms and Explosives stated in a 2011 letter that if a transferor knows that a potential transferee of a firearm possesses a card authorizing the possession and use of marijuana under state law, then the transferor has "reasonable cause to believe" that the person trying to get the firearm is an unlawful user of a controlled substance. The ATF further stated that "any person who uses or is addicted to marijuana, regardless of whether his or her State has passed legislation authorizing marijuana for medicinal purposes, is an unlawful user of or addicted to a controlled substance, and is prohibited by Federal law from possessing firearms or ammunition."

Knowingly transferring a firearm or ammunition to a user of illegal drugs is a felony. The maximum punishment in federal prison is ten years.

If you buy a gun, you have to fill out ATF Form 4473, Firearms Transaction Record. Question 11e asks, "Are you an unlawful user of, or addicted to, marijuana or any depressant, stimulant, narcotic drug, or any other controlled substance?" And right after that question, it has in bold print "Warning: The use or possession of marijuana remains unlawful under Federal law regardless of whether it has been legalized or decriminalized for medicinal or recreational purposes in the state where you reside." A gun seller may not legally sell a gun to anyone who checks "yes" to that question.

The bottom line is that you lose your gun rights if you use

marijuana—whether it's illegally or under a state-sanctioned medical marijuana program. Nobody may legally sell a gun or ammunition to someone they reasonably believe uses marijuana. Therefore, individuals seeking a medical marijuana license will have to weigh the risks and benefits of that course of action.

As more states legalize marijuana for both recreational and medicinal use, something clearly needs to give here. Oklahoma's approval of medical marijuana has been called a tipping point in the legalization of marijuana, and more states will follow. For now, however, it's a federal crime to own a gun and use marijuana, and it's a federal crime to transfer a gun to a marijuana user. The federal government must remove the threat of violating a federal law from otherwise law-abiding citizens and remove marijuana from the list of controlled substances.

SOURCES: 18 U.S.C. § 922, ATF Form 4473, 18 U.S.C. § 924, & ATF 2011 Letter

CAN I GET A GUN LICENSE IN OKLAHOMA IF I HAVE A MEDICAL MARIJUANA CARD?

Under the language enacted by SQ 788, a medical marijuana license holder may have and be issued a gun license. Section 245A in Title 63 of the Oklahoma Statutes states, "No person holding a medical marijuana license may unduly be withheld from holding a state issued license by virtue of their being a medical marijuana license holder. This would include such things as a concealed carry permit." A concealed carry permit is now referred to as a handgun permit.

It's believed that the new medical marijuana law overrides language in 21 O.S § 1290.10. It says that someone may not have a gun license if that person is ineligible to possess a pistol due to any provision of Oklahoma or U.S. law, except for felons who have been pardoned. Federal law states that anyone who is a user of a substance that the federal government considers illegal (which currently still includes marijuana) may not legally possess a gun or ammunition. Since this law is so new, the courts may ultimately have to decide this issue.

Even if you're allowed to get a gun permit as a medical

marijuana license holder under this new law, you still can't legally possess a firearm or ammunition. Firearms dealers may not sell a gun or ammunition to anyone they have reason to believe is an illegal drug user (per federal law). Possession of a medical marijuana license would give a firearms dealer sufficient reason to believe someone is an illegal drug user (under federal law).

Would The OSBI Or A Gun Dealer Know That I Have A Medical Marijuana License?

It is unlikely that the OSBI or firearms dealers would know whether you had a medical marijuana license. This is due to the protections in 63 O.S. § 420A. It states that "The State Department of Health will ensure that all application records and information are sealed to protect the privacy of medical license applicants." Therefore, we can assume that medical marijuana license information will remain private to everyone unless the individual discloses their status. The only way a firearms dealer would know that you have a medical marijuana license is if you told them about your medical marijuana license or used your medical marijuana license as a form of identification.

SOURCES: 18 U.S.C. § 922, ATF Form 4473, 18 U.S.C. §

924, & ATF 2011 Letter

DEFINITIONS

ADC – Area Defense Counsel

AFCF – After Former Conviction of a Felony

APC – Actual Physical Control

ARIDE – Advanced Roadside Impaired Driving Enforcement

ATF – Bureau of Alcohol, Tobacco, Firearms, and Explosives

CLEET – Council on Law Enforcement Education and Training

DRE – Drug Recognition Expert

DUI – Driving Under the Influence

DWI – Driving While Impaired

GOMOR – General Officer Memorandum of Reprimand

OSBI – Oklahoma State Bureau of Investigation

ROTC – Reserve Officer Training Corps

SFST – Standardized Field Sobriety Test

SQ – State Question

UCMJ – Uniform Code of Military Justice

DISCLAIMER

This publication is intended to be informational only. No legal advice is being given, and no attorney-client relationship is intended to be created by reading this material. If you are facing legal issues, whether criminal or civil, seek professional legal counsel to get your questions answered. The law cited is current as of September 1, 2018. Laws are subject to change at any time.

THE URBANIC LAW FIRM, PLLC
1141 N Robinson Avenue
Suite 101
Oklahoma City, OK 73103
(405) 633-3420

Frank@Urbanic.Law

www.Urbanic.Law

Made in United States
North Haven, CT
04 November 2026

21721416R00071